Pink Canvas

Dominique D. Glisson

Published by AfroSoFly Publishing, LLC.

Cover Design: "The Brain of Life" by Chris Anderson

Copyright © 2017 Dominique D. Glisson

All Rights Reserved

ISBN-13: 978-0-578-40669-5

Special thanks to my plethora of sisters,

Handpicked or biological,

I love you.

Table of Contents

A Love Letter to My Pussy .... *Coochie*

Vacancy .... *Pocketbook*

One Woman Fuck .... *Snatch*

Tropical Melody .... *Flower*

Daddii-Dick .... *Nookie*

Commando .... *Cookie*

Blank Check .... *Cherry*

The Artist .... *Jewel Box*

Interior Design .... *Breakfast of Champions*

Tea at 2 A.M. .... *Candy Kiss*

Untouchable .... *Pie*

For the Love of the D .... *Pum Pum*

Jealous .... *Pussy*

Abstinent .... *Cupcake*

Pipe Dream .... *Box*

Shit Like That .... *Pink Taco*

Heart .... *Camel Toe*

The Devil in Disguise .... *Na-Na*

Pure Negro .... *Yoni*

A Love Letter to My Pussy

Sweet thang,

Lips delicately folded like rose petals

You are dope.

You are as beautiful as you appear

So filled with fire

Juicy as sweet watermelon

You are rare.

You feed off your own energy

—life of your own party

You complete me.

Deflowered to perfection by few

You have mesmerized even them

Traces of your essence left on your lovers

Forces them to come back

Trouble maker, you are

A blessing and a curse

I do my best to pick the greatest lovers

But no one loves you like I do

I'd marry you.

Excited by my fingertips

You are so spoiled.

All day and night, you crave my touch

I yearn for your taste

Sweet; just like me

Long lapses between payments of gratitude

You make me give you "Brooklyn Love"

You cum hard and put me to sleep

My angel

You are my means of happiness

Give me the dopamine you capture

Confident in how desirable you make him feel

You tighten your already-tight walls

Around his shaft

You make him feel so attractive

You give him adrenaline

His stamina boosts to please you,

To please me

You're a team player

Pure and simple

Accustomed to his touch and mine,

You curve only to the shape of him

You purr for him and no one else

Remarkable chemistry between pussy and person

—you and me.

Highly addictive

You are always ready for love

Ready to be loved

Ready to love

Sweet thang, Eye love you.

Vacancy

There's been a recent vacancy in my throat

My tonsils are so alone

I can see how faithful women turn to women

I don't want to cheat on my man

—with another penis

I want a friend

He's always on the go and when I'm not,

I'm home—still,

I want someone to hold me

To wipe my tears and massage my scalp

Look up at me and kiss my lips, gently

I want a secure woman who wants to turn me out

A friend who'll be my backbone

As I maintain my position as his

Someone who'll take my calls

When work has him "too busy" to talk

A woman who invites me to her home

My friend—tell me it's too late to drive

Tuck me in,

Take me from my empty bottle of wine—

She'll kiss me goodnight and kiss her way down

Kiss between my thighs

Her lips on both sets of mine

We can devour me together

I'll exercise my tongue on her breasts

As I would on his corona

Had he been there, he could be here

—But it's just me.

One Woman Fuck

This is my fantasy so I'll switch up the vibe

Put everything on the table

and not leave a thing inside

Let's not walk into the room together

Meet me at the bar and question

My trench coat in 90-degree weather

I lean in, "Wouldn't you like to know?"

Then give you a key to suite 6-9-0

I leave.

As I ride the elevator to the sixth floor

I walk into my hotel suite, alone

I can smell the scent of your cologne

Clashing with my candles

Burning a strawberry fragrance

You enter.

I drop my coat and I'm damn near naked

My leather boots come up to my knees

I'm rockin' the shit out of my outfit

As you can see

A black one-piece, connected at the hip

You love this sight

I can tell by your dick

You ask if the zipper ever gets caught on my hair

I zip it down for you to discover

The coochie is bare.

My boobies sit upright

Demanding to be touched

Your penis is standing up

Demanding to be fucked

I sit you down, handcuffed to the desk

Then I realize I can't be turned on

Without the help of my guest

I unzip your pants and let my tongue work the middle

Pink Canvas *Kitty Kat*

I suck hard and lick your sack a little

My nipples are hard so I massage in circles

Dick still in mouth—

I stop...stand

Move to the bed and wait

I remove the plastic penis from the belt on my waist

I suck and drool, letting out little screams

Babies drip from your penis

Just from watching me

I put the plastic penis in my vagina

Deep strokes

You came all over your chair

Fuck! This vibration got me pullin' my own hair

I bust a good one all over this thing

Then suck it again, until it's good and clean!

Tropical Melody

This time love hit me like a wave

and I was nowhere near the ocean

I stood there wet

Soaked in juices from the most forbidden fruit

I couldn't dare pass up a chance to be bold

I dared to be different and now

I got a bad man

His symphonies cut the tartar and plaque on my heart

I've started a band

He's my musician of choice

In an effort to enhance the beauty

of his bass instrumental creativity

His piano driven fingers tame my spirit

As my soul dances to the rhythm of his words

Almighty king of the symbols

Pink Canvas *Vagina*

Pap-pap

The harmonious sound of love making

He soaks himself

In the juices of my forbidden fruit

Daring to be bold

I'm surfing this wave of love and still—

I'm nowhere near the ocean.

Daddii-Dick

Sex feels natural to me

Yet here I am, on a bid of abstinence

It's like right now

I see penis every time I open

Close or even blink my eyes

All of the other cars in traffic

Turn into Daddii-Dick mobiles

My music bumps the 90s jams

I get to grindin' in my seat and singing like I wrote

Then I start *sangin'*—like when I rode it

Daddii-Dick tips rubbed on my clit

If I cum behind this wheel, I'm going to crash

Faces replaced with Daddii-Dick heads—

For every name I don't know

Daddii-Dick on my phone

Pink Canvas *Lady Parts*

Daddii-Dick on my mind

Daddii-Dick everywhere but where it needs to be—

Obviously inside of me

Spread across the dinner table; cummin' on the wood

Fuck.

I'm spaced out in my own space;

Cummin' on my fingers, instead

Commando

I feel with the forces of my vagina

and when she feels good

All is peaches and pie—

Sweet potato pie

Unbound by the cotton of panties

I feel free to conquer,

Free to engage

The key to my heart is buried in my vagina

Cervix deep and what you find

Is still mine to keep

Firewall protection

Security is tight

Pardon my aggression

Panties restrict my better nature

Follicles love fresh air

Day and night breeze

Makes it easy for me to breathe

Blank Check

Someone gave me good advice

"When you see someone down and out,

no matter how much you love them,

Leave them where they're at!

Don't take on that burden."

I took on you.

I gave you everything

I guess that's the problem

I set you up to be great;

and you didn't have to earn any of it

I didn't make you work for it

I thought that loving me was hard work enough

Where is my self-esteem?

I go hard for broken daughters—

Always forgetting I have my own shattered mirrors

Pink Canvas   *Poontang*

I thought

You loving me…was like giving me a blank check

I'd fill in the voids

with my hope for dreams and prosperity;

I'll support you on your journey

to leading my life as I lead you that way

You led me to the bank

Personal checks don't clear right away

and you cashed out on a check I can't cash…damn!

The Artist

Let's paint a picture

Using none other than the artistic brush

First things first:

Get it nice and wet

Position the canvas to an angle that suits you best

Start by using only the tip

Gently stroke the canvas up and down

Get some side strokes going

Hit that circular motion

Be creative

Tease the canvas

Alternate the direction in which you take

Work in one spot before expanding

Never taking on more than you can handle

or else it will be disastrous

Pink Canvas *Chocha*

Don't rush

Pace your gentle strokes

A masterpiece—

Takes time.

Any paint job can be completed

But this particular canvas

Needs wet paint to thrive

Effort and diligence

The masterpiece—

Takes form and creates a work of its own

Interior Design

Indiscriminately

Fuckin to repair the damaged goods that I am

Like a dented car or a faded hot cereal tin

In the grocery store

Taken home because my insides

Are fulfilling and wholesome

Sweet, juicy, and for the taking

Of select clean knights with huge armor

Hurting those who get too close

Beyond perimeters of touch

Hurting me

As I envision a man who isn't present

Auctioning time

Paid with pain-free vaginal spasms

Outburst flooding my interior design

Pink Canvas *Pudding*

Created from intriguing materials

New York

Cutting-edge, yet so beautiful

New York

Minutes racing against the heart that stopped

By way of the train equipped not to choo

No coal

No smoke

Tracks laid to ride

Selfless acts performed with my backside

Flexed

Twisted and bent

Comfort leaves faster

than a New York minute

Pink Canvas   *Privates*

Afterbirth lasted longer than my

Numerous trips to ecstasy

Cloud 9 has never appeared so gritty

Grimy

Broken

Tea at 2 A.M.

I got love for him

But I'm not in love with him

Sometimes I think I am—mid stroke

Tongue kiss and choke

But when he goes

I don't yearn for him until my body calls

Pussy…pussy throbbin'

Waiting up for love at 2 A.M. with my tea

Dummy box sounding off in the background

Memories of beauty and imagery of deceit

Once again, my mind is at war

—with my vagina

Cool touch on a late summer night

Toes curled under the throw

Chamomile to soothe my throat

Pink Canvas *Sweet Spot*

Sore from the pleasures of the night before

Tonsils as red as the stain

As the lips that left the gloss on his briefs

Lemon drops and honey

Slow sips

The dick won't let me leave

Untouchable

Sitting in psychology, horny as ever

Thinking crazy thoughts

I can't seem to get it together

What if I had a friend that did everything I asked

and if he never touches me,

Will my boyfriend get mad?

He says it's okay to fantasize

Look, not with your hands

Use your eyes

At least that's his excuse

For being where he was

But what if I invited a guest

To see me do what I does?

What if I walk into a room

Sit my guest on the bed

Pink Canvas   *Vajayjay*

Walk over to a chair and pull my shirt over my head

Stimulating my breasts

Soon to step out of my skirt

To let him see the rest

The rules are strictly 'DO NOT TOUCH'

As I lively present to him

The one woman fuck

I caress my breast slowly with my hands

I arch my back

One hand on my tit, on finger in my mouth

I lubricate the finger to send it down south

Up and down, side to side

My fingers bring my clit to life

I moan as I increase my speed

I see him growing in his jeans

My head tilts, fingers insert

—class dismissed.

For the Love of the D

He smiles beautifully

Thinks of me

Stands tall, dark, handsome

Muscular, educated and witty

Dedicates his existence

To the *me* that I am

Similar to the ME he knows

Cold—

Shielded by the walls of destruction

I noticed him smiling at me

I fit into the gap between his teeth

Yearning for him to fill the gap

Between my cheeks

I'm obsessed with what I now see

A donkey dick

Would wet my panties

If only I wore them around him

Romance—

Not of interest to me

He has committed himself

To a woman who just wants to fuck

A woman who has twice been fucked

Without permission

A woman who lets an orgasm

Replace the space of affection

A woman

Me

To keep me is to love me

From a distance

His embrace is warm, strong

Delicate to my fears

Semen in me

Early morning Plan-B

Love—

Only felt for what comes from me

He's so close to me

I care—

I want nothing to happen to his penis

Pleasure this fantastic is worth keeping

We connect

Spiritually, for him

Sexually, for me

Jealous

My vagina is jealous of the body in which it resides

If she could distance herself off to an island, she would

She'd detach herself from her connected womb

For the womb, she says, requires way too much

"Feed her life and shower her with love."

All things my vagina supports

But what about what SHE needs?

Girth and length; Fondle, stroke, and kiss.

She can't have a good time for just one night

Without subjecting her to the dangers of that life

Capped, hooded, and raw—hitting so close to home

Trolling down Womb Street through Vagina Turnpike

My vagina has to be broken now that she is not in use

Pink Canvas   *Rosebud*

My personality has diminished

I look in the mirror and I see the remains of her

So far off from how vibrant she once was

Lost in what feels like my second virginity

This cannot be life

Consciously deciding to withhold penis from myself

The nerve of my clitoris to smile at the wind

Abstinent

The harmonious sound of your heartbeat is fading

My heart is dancing slowly

Trying hard to regain the rhythm that once was

Or a hint of bass it could still be

Last call...I can't feel my toes

Shall I clutch my purse and leave?

Lip gloss...check!

Mascara...check!

Keys...check!

Phone...lock screen. Wait!

DJ, please run that song back

Cut it until it scratches and permanently begins again

and again and again

The lights are on and I look pathetic

I feel...my feet hurt

Pipe Dream

My love is impatiently patient

Frustrations of waiting

Legs closed

Heart opened

Twat untouched

Fuck me—

Shitless

Fiber-fuck me

To the heavens of bowels

Plumb through

and lay pipe!

Unsealed leaks

Faucet overflow

Shit.

Shit Like That

My sex drive is insatiable

Even on my most fulfilled days

I can't keep my fingers off and out of my pussy

Cummin at 12 plays

Twelve videos at six minutes or more

No longer horny, just yearning

Sensations of His reaching of my vagina's back door

Making my pussy climax with force

I'm greedy

All alone at work and feeling hella needy

I need to bounce up on it

Just one more time

My vagina strives to be plunged

Pink Canvas *Clitoris*

Punish me for my appetite

Give me more than nine

Tear me apart with all you've got

Make me run, and red…make her swell

Again and again

Give me that kinda D

That makes me forget I'm asleep

As I rest in peace

Heart

Evolve with me

Hold down the revolver with me

Should shit go south

Climb back up to the top

—with me.

Eye need you in my life with me

Your heart's no longer cold and closed

Your heart is in my back pocket

—with me.

Look at me with closed eyes

Use your ears to study the rhythm of my heart

Let your heartbeat sync with mine

And every time

You penetrate and leave your trace

Ecstasy hits my blood stream

Do you see me with the love that I do?

The Devil in Disguise

The devil is a liar

The devil is no oil

to fry the seasoned chicken

No honey to put in the tea

For dinner tonight

The devil is the cop at your door

Telling you your oldest son is dead

While raiding your home for drugs

Or the cop that sits

In the bushes while you ride

Past the speed limit

Pulls you over

to give you a ticket

The devil is when you're a black man

Being arrested

For "fitting the description"

When you show up to work

With slippers on your feet

When you're in class

and can't hide

The growling in your stomach

Can't hide the flatulence

From the morning's eggs

The devil is the 12-year-old

Who has sex with no conscience—

Because she was molested when she was 8

The English language

Well spoken over the phone

The priceless expression

When they see you're black

The rain when you step out of the salon

Pink Canvas *Pearl*

The devil is the stray bullet

In the heart of an innocent child

At the hand of a corrupted public servant

A conscious mind turned off

Corns in open-toe shoes

Pure Negro

Negro gal with Negro hair

Negro child with Negro cares

Negro face for Negro fears

Negro nose breathes Negro air

Negro daddy gives Negro features

Negro funds buy Negro sneakers

Negro love for non-Negro creatures

Negro often misled by Negro preachers

Negro tongue speaks Negro truth

Negro brain powered by Negro juice

Negro womb bearing Negro fruit

Negro skin heals every Negro bruise

Pink Canvas *Garden*

Negro soul reflected in Negro eyes

Negro pussy protected by Negro thighs

Negro lows uplifted by Negro highs

Negro truth buried deep in Negro lies

Negro strength tested against Negro blows

Negro flesh beneath Negro clothes

Negro naps projected in Negro fros

Negro lives a life only a Negro knows

www.ingramcontent.com/pod-product-compliance
Lightning Source LLC
Chambersburg PA
CBHW021413290426
44108CB00010B/514